PHILI

MW01057956

A Letter to
Friends

A Guided Discovery for Groups and Individuals

Kevin Perrotta

LOYOLAPRESS.

CHICAGO

LOYOLAPRESS.

3441 N. Ashland Avenue
CHICAGO, ILLINOIS 60657

Imprimatur
Most Reverend Raymond E. Goedert,
    M.A., S.T.L., J.C.L.
Vicar General
Archdiocese of Chicago
August 21, 2001

Nihil Obstat
Carolyn Osiek, R.S.C.J.
Censor Deputatus
August 18, 2001

The *Nihil Obstat* and *Imprimatur* are official declarations that a book is free of doctrinal and moral error. No implication is contained therein that those who have granted the *Nihil Obstat* and *Imprimatur* agree with the content, opinions, or statements expressed.

The Scripture quotations contained herein are from the New Revised Standard Version Bible: Catholic Edition, copyright © 1993 and 1989 by the Division of Christian Education of the National Council of the Churches of Christ in the U.S.A. Used by permission. All rights reserved. Subheadings in Scripture quotations have been added by Kevin Perrotta.

The excerpt from St. Francis de Sales (p. 40) is from Henry Benedict Mackey, trans., *Library of St. Francis de Sales,* vol. 5 (London: Burns, Oates, and Washbourne, 1923), 412–13.

The excerpt on page 60 is from Louise Perrotta, *The Saints' Guide to Learning to Pray* (Ann Arbor, Mich.: Servant Books, 2001).

The Latin text of the comments by St. Thomas Aquinas (p. 61) may be found in S. Thomae Aquinatis, *In Omnes S. Pauli Apostoli Epistolas Commentaria,* vol. 1 (Turin: Libraria Marietti, 1929), 98–106. Translation by Kevin Perrotta.

Interior design by Kay Hartmann/Communique Design
Illustration by Charise Mericle

ISBN 0-8294-1568-8

Printed in the United States of America
01 02 03 04 05 06 07 08 09 Bang 9 8 7 6 5 4 3 2 1

Contents

How to Use This Guide

Y ou might compare the Bible to a national park. The park is so large that you could spend months, even years, getting to know it. But a brief visit, if carefully planned, can be enjoyable and worthwhile. In a few hours you can drive through the park and pull over at a handful of sites. At each stop you can get out of the car, take a short trail through the woods, listen to the wind blowing through the trees, get a feel for the place.

In this booklet we'll read the letter of St. Paul to the Christian community at Philippi. Because the letter is short, we'll be able to take a leisurely walk through it, thinking carefully about what we are reading and what it means for our lives today. Although the letter is short, it gives us a great deal to reflect on, for Paul packed it with a tremendous amount of insight into God's love for us and the life he calls us to live.

This guide provides everything you need to explore Philippians in six discussions—or to do a six-part exploration on your own. The introduction on page 6 will prepare you to get the most out of your reading. The weekly sections provide explanations that highlight what Paul's words mean for us today. Equally important, each section supplies questions that will launch you into fruitful discussion, helping you to both investigate the letter for yourself and learn from one another. If you're using the booklet by yourself, the questions will spur your personal reflection.

Each discussion is meant to be a *guided discovery.*

Guided. None of us is equipped to read the Bible without help. We read the Bible *for* ourselves but not *by* ourselves. Scripture was written to be understood and applied in the community of faith. So each week "A Guide to the Reading," drawing on the work of both modern biblical scholars and Christian writers of the past, supplies background and explanations. The guide will help you grasp the message of Philippians. Think of it as a friendly park ranger who points out noteworthy details and explains what you're looking at so you can appreciate things for yourself.

Discovery. The purpose is for *you* to interact with this New Testament letter. "Questions for Careful Reading" is a tool to help you dig into the text and examine it carefully. "Questions for

Application" will help you consider what these words mean for your life here and now. Each week concludes with an "Approach to Prayer" section that helps you respond to God's word. Supplementary "Living Tradition" and "Saints in the Making" sections offer the thoughts and experiences of Christians past and present. By showing what this letter has meant to others, these sections will help you consider what it means for you.

How long are the discussion sessions? We've assumed you will have about an hour and a half when you get together. If you have less time, you'll find that most of the elements can be shortened somewhat.

Is homework necessary? You will get the most out of your discussions if you read the weekly material and prepare your answers to the questions in advance of each meeting. If participants are not able to prepare, have someone read the "Guide to the Reading" sections aloud at the points where they appear.

What about leadership? If you happen to have a world-class biblical scholar in your group, by all means ask him or her to lead the discussions. In the absence of any professional Scripture scholars, or even accomplished biblical amateurs, you can still have a first-class Bible discussion. Choose two or three people to take turns as facilitators, and have everyone read "Suggestions for Bible Discussion Groups" (page 76) before beginning.

Does everyone need a guide? a Bible? Everyone in the group will need their own copy of this booklet. The booklet contains the entire text of Philippians, so a Bible is not absolutely necessary—but each participant will find it useful to have one. You should have at least one Bible on hand for your discussions. (See page 80 for recommendations.)

How do we get started? Before you begin, take a look at the suggestions for Bible discussion groups (page 76) or individuals (page 79).

A Warm and Challenging Friendship

As Christians, we read the Bible for one reason above all: to deepen our knowledge of Jesus. True, the Gospels, which provide us with most of our scriptural evidence of Jesus' life, account for less than half the total length even of the New Testament. Yet the Gospels are only one means of access to Jesus. The Old Testament forms the background for understanding Jesus. The writings that follow the Gospels in the New Testament convey what the early Church believed about him. Equally important, these New Testament writings show the transforming effect he had on his followers after his death and resurrection. This evidence of his impact on their lives helps us grasp not only who he is but also who he wishes to be for us.

St. Paul's letter to the Philippians gives us a vivid impression of the early Christians' experience of Jesus. In this letter Paul speaks quite openly about himself, allowing us to glimpse his love for his Lord. Paul's encouragements to the believers in Philippi are marked by a warmth that is unmarred by the reproaches he felt obliged to make in his letters to some other Christian communities. This is an openhearted letter, a letter between friends about their relationship with their mutual friend, Jesus.

Someone said that Christianity is not so much taught as caught: we pick it up through contact with Christians. I am reminded of how I have learned about marriage. Much has come to me simply from being around married couples—first my parents and grandparents and aunts and uncles, then other couples over the years. I have learned about respect in marriage from hearing spouses speak to each other in tones of appreciation, even admiration, and without sarcasm. Some spouses have been living lessons in mutual trust. Some have demonstrated the possibility of enduring romance by their manner with each other even after decades of living together. Similarly, our relationship with Jesus can be nourished by hanging around Paul and the Philippians and observing how they relate to Jesus and to one another—how they pray for one another, how they support one another, how they are sensitive to one another's feelings. We can find in this letter not only instructions about Christian beliefs but also an instructive picture of how Jesus was reshaping Paul's and the Philippians' lives.

To grasp the spiritual dynamics of Paul's and the Philippians' lives, it is useful to have some idea of their circumstances and the events that led up to the letter. Here is a little background:

Philippi was a city in northern Greece. In the first century, it was a Roman "colony." This did not mean it was a settlement in a wild or thinly populated land. Roman colonies were cities that were established in well-populated districts in the empire and consisted of Roman soldiers and others with ties to the imperial regime. The colonies were designed to anchor their areas in loyalty to Rome. Many of the residents of the colonies held Roman citizenship, a privilege that belonged to only a small minority of people in the empire. The colonists followed Roman law and religion as though they lived in Rome itself. As a colony, Philippi was a kind of branch office of Rome, Inc., representing Roman interests in northern Greece.

For a short time, Paul was a Jewish leader who persecuted the earliest Christian community in Jerusalem. A few years after Jesus' death and resurrection, Paul received a vision of the risen Jesus that convinced him that Jesus is the promised Messiah who offers life in the Spirit not only to Jewish people but to everyone (Acts 9:1–19; 22:21). Paul first visited Philippi on a missionary trip around the year A.D. 50. As background for the letter, a narrative of Paul's first visit to Philippi is included in our reading for Week 1. It is taken from the Acts of the Apostles, which was written by St. Luke, who apparently accompanied Paul in Philippi (page 13). Paul made many missionary journeys, planted churches, and stayed in touch with them by letters, several of which have survived and are included in the New Testament.

We do not know how long Paul stayed in Philippi, but after he left, the Christian community there continued to grow, even though the Christians faced opposition from their fellow townspeople. The community would sometimes send Paul financial support for his missionary travels (see 2 Corinthians 8:1–4; the Philippians are among the "Macedonians" Paul describes there).

Paul writes to the Philippians while he is in legal custody awaiting trial. Since his Philippian friends know where he is and why he is being tried, he does not need to state these matters in the letter—to the frustration of later readers, who have been left to conjecture about Paul's whereabouts and the timing of the letter. Scholars have proposed various theories, the most satisfactory of which is that he is in Rome, toward the end of the period of detention described in Acts 28:16–31. (We will read an excerpt from this account in Week 2—page 23.) As he writes, Paul is nearing the end of some four years of custody. The date is A.D. 61, give or take a year.

It seems that Paul is not being held in excessively severe conditions. Acts pictures him under house arrest. He is allowed to receive financial gifts and have visitors. At the same time, he is not a prominent or powerful person whose social connections might protect him from all the disagreeable aspects of detention.

In general, the Roman state did not supply necessities to prisoners. It was up to their family and friends to provide them with food and clothing. So Paul must have been glad when a man named Epaphroditus, a member of the Christian community in Philippi, arrived in Rome with a financial gift from the Philippians. In those days, the trip from Philippi to Rome was hardly a snap, although it was relatively uncomplicated by ancient standards. The traveler, typically on foot, would proceed west from Philippi on the Roman main road for a couple of hundred miles, would cross the Adriatic Sea by ship, and would then complete an equally long stretch of road north through Italy—about forty days' travel, one way. It seems that Epaphroditus became seriously ill en route and almost died after reaching Rome.

This brings us to our letter. Paul is writing to the Philippians to thank them for their financial support and to commend Epaphroditus, who is returning to Philippi bearing the letter. Naturally, Paul includes news about himself, as well as advice, warnings, and encouragements.

The Philippians' situation cannot be reconstructed in detail. This is due to a lack of historical sources. But we can make some inferences from the letter itself. The Philippians are facing several challenges:

External opposition. As Christians, the Philippian believers recognize Jesus as "Lord" and "Savior" (2:11; 3:20; all references are to Philippians unless otherwise noted). This puts them at odds with their city, which as a Roman colony prides itself on its loyalty to Caesar, who is called "lord" and "savior"—titles that express political and religious commitment. Christians' refusal to worship the emperor as divine looks like political disloyalty. Pagan residents of the city would see Christianity, with its different Lord and its legally unrecognized network of loyalties, as a blot on their city's special relationship with the imperial government. At this point there is no indication that any of the Christians are facing martyrdom. More likely they are experiencing social and economic pressures from their pagan relatives, friends, clients, customers, business colleagues, masters (almost certainly some members of the community are household slaves), and government officials (1:28–30).

Internal friction. Paul's appeals for unity and harmony (1:27; 2:1–2, 14) suggest that the community's cohesion is threatened. At one point he specifically begs two of the leading women in the community to be reconciled with each other (4:2). How serious is the problem? Biblical scholar Peter O'Brien observes that "there is no severity of censure in Paul's words, and this suggests that the divisions or dissension had not yet reached an acute stage. Yet the frequency and urgency of the apostle's appeals imply that the danger of disruption was real." Paul is concerned enough that he is willing to forego the presence of his right-hand man, Timothy, in order to find out how things are going with the Philippians (2:19).

Misguided Christian-Jewish missionaries. Because of its location on a main road, Philippi is undoubtedly visited by travelers spreading various brands of Christianity. The Philippians probably offer hospitality to all and sundry. Some of the missionaries argue that Christians from a pagan background, such as the Philippians, need to complete their conversion to God by becoming Jews and keeping the whole Mosaic law, including the rules of dietary and ceremonial purity, the Sabbath, and male circumcision. As we will see in the guides to the reading (and the brief essay on page 74), the approach of these Judaizing Christian missionaries was a serious problem. It is not certain that any of these missionaries are present in Philippi as Paul writes, but he knows of the danger from his work with other local churches. We can infer the importance of the problem in Paul's mind from the fact that he devotes a considerable portion of the letter to making a case against these missionaries (chapter 3).

Meanwhile at Rome, many Christians are becoming more outspoken in their efforts to make Jesus known to the people around them (1:14). But clouds of persecution are gathering on the horizon. The Romans had mixed feelings about foreign religions and sometimes resisted introduction of them into their city. They regarded imported religions as "superstitions" and feared they would jeopardize the relationship between Rome and its gods that made the city secure. Within three or four years of Paul's writing to the Philippians, a great fire will ravage the city of Rome. Rumors will spread that the emperor Nero set the blaze to clear the way for his personal building projects. To deflect these suspicions from himself, Nero will make the Christians scapegoats. Some of the Christians in Rome whom Paul commends in his letter for their evangelistic efforts will be swept away in a savage persecution.

And what of Paul? It is likely that he was released soon after completing the letter. Possibly he then traveled east for a visit to Philippi and other cities where he had founded Christian communities. According to a well-founded tradition, he returned to Rome (biblical scholar Jerome Murphy-O'Connor surmises he went back to support the Roman Christians who were suffering persecution). Before long, Paul was seized and executed. His martyrdom and that of Peter at about the same time in Rome made the city one of the earliest places of Christian pilgrimage, as believers came to pray at the tombs of these two great leaders of the early Church.

Paul's letter to the Philippians poses a challenge to us. The Christians in Philippi were deeply committed to advancing the gospel, even at great personal cost. Most of us would admit that we do not live at their level of faith and self-sacrificing service to others. We might honestly say that we are not sure we *want* to have our lives centered so completely on Jesus and his cause in the world. Reading Philippians is like meeting a saintly person: you find something about the person very appealing, yet also very disturbing, for even without the person saying a word, the person's life confronts you with the question "Why shouldn't you be a saint too?"

If you feel this kind of disturbance as you read Philippians, don't brush it off. Maybe it is a sign of the Holy Spirit. If you wonder how to respond constructively, you will discover much in the letter that will aid your reflection. Paul urges us to set Jesus as the goal of our lives and to direct everything toward him, and Paul offers himself as a model. "Forgetting what lies behind and straining forward to what lies ahead, I press on toward the goal for the prize of the heavenly call of God in Christ Jesus" (3:13–14). Yet Paul emphasizes that our striving for Jesus is only a response to God's grace. God "has graciously granted . . . the privilege . . . of believing in Christ" (1:29). God is at work in us, enabling us "both to will and to work for his good pleasure" (2:13). It is God's power, displayed in Jesus' resurrection (3:10), that will make us be as he is (3:21).

Paul is well aware that responding to Christ is not a single event but a lifelong process. He prays for the Philippians to grow "more and more" in love (1:9). He recognizes that he himself has not arrived in the spiritual life ("not that I have already . . . reached the goal"—3:12). As for the Philippians, although they set a high standard of laboring for Christ, they too have a ways to go. At the moment of Paul's writing, two of their most stalwart members are locked in conflict with each other (4:2–3).

The Christian life, whether in first-century Philippi or in twenty-first-century Fresno, is empowered by Christ. Because Christ has made us his own (see 3:12), whatever the challenges we face or the weaknesses we confront in ourselves, we can "rejoice in the Lord" (4:4).

A Lot to Be Thankful For

Questions to Begin

15 minutes
Use a question or two to get warmed up for the reading.

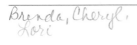

1 To whom are you especially grateful for help in a time of need?

---

2 Have you ever lived through an earthquake? If not, what memorable disaster have you experienced?

5 minutes
Read the passage aloud. Let individuals take turns reading
paragraphs.

The Reading: Acts 16:13–40; Philippians 1:1–11

The Beginnings of the Church in Philippi

Acts 16:13 On the sabbath day we went outside the gate by the river, where we supposed there was a place of prayer; and we sat down and spoke to the women who had gathered there. 14 A certain woman named Lydia, a worshiper of God, was listening to us; she was from the city of Thyatira and a dealer in purple cloth. The Lord opened her heart to listen eagerly to what was said by Paul. 15 When she and her household were baptized, she urged us, saying, "If you have judged me to be faithful to the Lord, come and stay at my home." And she prevailed upon us.

16 One day, as we were going to the place of prayer, we met a slave-girl who had a spirit of divination and brought her owners a great deal of money by fortune-telling. 17 While she followed Paul and us, she would cry out, "These men are slaves of the Most High God, who proclaim to you a way of salvation." 18 . . . But Paul, very much annoyed, turned and said to the spirit, "I order you in the name of Jesus Christ to come out of her." And it came out that very hour.

19 But when her owners saw that their hope of making money was gone, they seized Paul and Silas and dragged them into the marketplace before the authorities. 20 When they had brought them before the magistrates, they said, "These men are disturbing our city; they are Jews 21 and are advocating customs that are not lawful for us as Romans to adopt or observe." 22 The crowd joined in attacking them, and the magistrates had them stripped of their clothing and ordered them to be beaten with rods. 23 After they had given them a severe flogging, they threw them into prison. . . .

25 About midnight Paul and Silas were praying and singing hymns to God, and the prisoners were listening to them. 26 Suddenly there was an earthquake, so violent that the foundations of the prison were shaken; and immediately all the doors were opened and every-one's chains were unfastened. 27 When the jailer woke up and saw the prison doors wide open, he drew his sword and was about to kill himself, since he supposed that the prisoners had escaped. 28 But Paul shouted in a loud voice, "Do not harm yourself, for we are all here." 29 The jailer called for lights, and rushing in, he fell down trembling

before Paul and Silas. 30 Then he brought them outside and said, "Sirs, what must I do to be saved?" 31 They answered, "Believe on the Lord Jesus, and you will be saved, you and your household." 32 They spoke the word of the Lord to him and to all who were in his house. 33 At the same hour of the night he took them and washed their wounds; then he and his entire family were baptized without delay. 34 He brought them up into the house and set food before them; and he and his entire household rejoiced that he had become a believer in God.

35 When morning came, the magistrates sent the police, saying, "Let those men go." . . . 40 After leaving the prison they went to Lydia's home; and when they had seen and encouraged the brothers and sisters there, they departed.

A Decade Later, a Letter to the Philippians

Philippians 1:1 Paul and Timothy, servants of Christ Jesus,

To all the saints in Christ Jesus who are in Philippi, with the bishops and deacons:

2 Grace to you and peace from God our Father and the Lord Jesus Christ.

3 I thank my God every time I remember you, 4 constantly praying with joy in every one of my prayers for all of you, 5 because of your sharing in the gospel from the first day until now. 6 I am confident of this, that the one who began a good work among you will bring it to completion by the day of Jesus Christ. 7 It is right for me to think this way about all of you, because you hold me in your heart, for all of you share in God's grace with me, both in my imprisonment and in the defense and confirmation of the gospel. 8 For God is my witness, how I long for all of you with the compassion of Christ Jesus. 9 And this is my prayer, that your love may overflow more and more with knowledge and full insight 10 to help you to determine what is best, so that in the day of Christ you may be pure and blameless, 11 having produced the harvest of righteousness that comes through Jesus Christ for the glory and praise of God.

Questions for Careful Reading

10 minutes
Choose questions according to your interest and time.
(The questions refer only to the reading from Philippians.)

He is thanking God for Philippian Church
Keeping on the path for
Christ

1 Paul is thankful (1:3). What exactly does he thank God for?

Holy Spirit, work in our life
Conforming us to the likeness
of Jesus.

2 Who began the good work in verse 6? What work did he begin?

Paul is their shepard
Like Jesus was Pauls
Paul loves them (Phillippians)

3 Identify Paul's references to Jesus in this passage. What does his frequent mention of Jesus suggest about Paul and his relationship with the Philippians?

That his connections of
Jesus were very strong
Great faith

4 If you knew nothing about Paul, what impression of him would you get from this section of his letter?

5 In everyday terms, what does it mean to live "for the glory and praise of God" (1:11)?

A Guide to the Reading

If participants have not read this section already, read it aloud. Otherwise go on to "Questions for Application."

Acts 16:13–40. The excerpt from Acts tells how the Christian community in Philippi began and introduces its first members— Lydia and her household and the director of the city's jail and his family. Paul does not single them out in the letter we are about to read. But they are probably present when his letter arrives and is read aloud at the community's weekly meeting. Possibly the community is still gathering in Lydia's home (verse 40).

Philippians 1:1–2. Some ten to twelve years have passed since the events in Acts 16. Paul now writes from Rome to the Christians in Philippi. He addresses "the bishops and deacons" (or "overseers and ministers") in particular, for they will have a special responsibility to lead the community in responding to his instruction. But he will not mention the leaders again. Paul writes to the whole community (count the instances when he speaks of "all" and "every" member in this week's reading alone). Each member of the church in Philippi—and each of us—must pay attention to his message and put it into practice.

1:3–5. At this point, an ancient letter-writer would offer a wish for the recipient's well-being—usually a quick "I hope everything's okay with you" (3 John 2 is an example). The length of Paul's report on his hopes for the Philippians (1:3–11) is a measure of his friendship with them.

Paul thanks God not mainly for what the Philippians have done for Paul but for what they have been doing *with* Paul *for* Christ. They have been "sharing" in the gospel (1:5). The Greek word means "participation"; the Philippians have been taking part with Paul in the Christian mission. The "gospel" here means the announcing of the message about Jesus. (The "first day" [1:5] of the gospel was the initial announcement of Jesus in Philippi that we just read about in Acts 16.) Thus Paul is not saying merely that the Philippians accepted the message about Jesus but that they have been working actively to bring this message to others. After Paul left Philippi, the Philippians continued to communicate with people about Jesus, even though they themselves had become Christians only recently. One scholar remarks, "This text provides a fine biblical example of the 'apostolate of the laity.'"

1:6. While Paul is glad for the Philippians' efforts, he knows that Christian life springs from a source deeper than human determination. Our service to God is an outgrowth of God's "good work" in us. God both initiates the good we do and brings it to accomplishment.

1:7–8. (These verses are a kind of parenthetical addition. Try skipping them at first, reading directly from verse 6 to verse 9.) "Because you hold me in your heart" could also be translated "because I hold you in my heart." Paul and the Philippians are fond of each other because they have the experience of "being in this Christian-mission thing together." The Philippians have been loyal to Paul during his imprisonment, even though it was an embarrassment to them. But notice that Paul has confidence that God will complete his work in them (1:6) not primarily because of their labors or their loyalty to Paul but because they "share in God's grace." Paul's hope is based not on their faithfulness but on God's.

1:9–11. Paul resumes his report on his prayer for the Philippians that he began in verses 3 and 4. He hopes that they will live in expectation of the coming of God's kingdom. "Paul's prayer is that they might live the life of the future in the present," comments New Testament scholar Gordon D. Fee. For most of us, the final coming of God's kingdom seems so far off that we find it difficult to orient our lives toward it. But Paul points out the incremental means by which we can direct our lives toward God's kingdom—by growing in love. If we grow in love, we will increasingly be able "to determine what is best" (1:10). This means more than knowing which job to take or what to cook for dinner. It means being able to discern what is important, having insight into what really counts, grasping what is essential for living toward God's kingdom. By growing in love, we will be able to see life more and more from an eternal perspective—from God's point of view. Plus, if we grow in love, we will have "knowledge" and "insight" (1:9)—the practical good judgment to know how to handle the various situations we face. We will become fruit trees heavy with fruit (1:11).

Questions for Application

40 minutes
Choose questions according to your interest and time.

1 How might Paul's prayer for the Philippians be a model for your prayer for your children or other members of your family? for the people in your parish? for others?

2 Compare yourself with Paul in verse 8. Do you tend to forget about people who need you to stay in touch with them? Who? What should you do about this?

3 In verse 9, Paul speaks of a connection between love and knowledge. Would Paul agree with the popular saying that love is blind? In what ways is love blind? In what ways does love help a person see more clearly?

4 Paul prays that the Philippians' love would "overflow more and more" (1:9). What does it mean for love to overflow? Where do you unconsciously or consciously draw the line and say to yourself, "I am not going to love more than that"? Where is God inviting you to let love overflow?

5 Paul was able to look beyond his own needs and encourage other people even when he was in a difficult situation. Who have you known like this? What can you learn from that person?

6 In what ways do you participate in bringing the gospel to other people? How does your parish do this? What step could you and your parish take to do it more?

7 In what area of your life is verse 6 a word for you? What does it say to you? What could you do to keep this word in mind in that situation?

Accept the fact that you do not know much. Being "biblically challenged" is nothing to be ashamed of!

Steve Mueller, *The Seeker's Guide to Reading the Bible*

Approach to Prayer

15 minutes
Use this approach—or create your own!

◆ Read aloud this observation
on this week's reading from
biblical scholar Gordon Fee:

Paul . . . rarely thanks God for
"things"; his thanksgivings are for
people, for those special "gifts"
whom God has brought into his
life, who, despite whatever
frustration or grief they may also
cause him, are invariably a source
of great joy and thanksgiving.

Take a few minutes for participants—either silently or
aloud, as they wish—to thank
God for the people through
whom he has touched their lives
and is touching others' lives,
and to pray for those people.

Pray an Our Father. Close
by asking someone to read
Philippians 1:6 aloud as a final
blessing for the group: "I am
confident of this, that the one
who began a good work among
you will bring it to completion
by the day of Jesus Christ."

Saints in the Making

A Short Course in Christianity

This section is a supplement for individual reading.

The cooperation between Paul and the Philippians in spreading the gospel has not always been imitated by later generations of Christians. In some periods, priests and religious have been not only the main agents for spreading the gospel, but seemingly almost the only ones. The twentieth century, however, saw a renaissance of evangelizing by laymen and laywomen.

An instructive example of priests and laypeople working together in evangelization is a movement called the Cursillo, which originated in Spain in the late 1940s. A group of priests and young laymen on the island of Majorca became deeply concerned for fellow Catholics for whom Christianity seemed to make little difference in ordinary life. A businessman, Eduardo Bonnin; a theology student, Juan Capo; and a priest, Sebastian Gaya, developed a method of reaching out to these men and women. They targeted those who seemed to be the natural leaders in their everyday environments and invited them to a three-day evangelistic retreat: a short course—in Spanish, a *cursillo*—in Christianity. Through brief talks and personal stories, most given by laypeople, the weekend helped participants make contact with Jesus as a living person who was calling them to give their lives to him in service to others. Participants who experienced a conversion through the retreat were then linked together in a network of small groups in which they supported one another in being "apostles" to their social environments of business, government, education, and so on.

During the forties and fifties, the Cursillo movement spread in Spanish-speaking countries; in the sixties it began to attract English-speaking Catholics in the United States. Over almost a half-century, the movement has profoundly affected thousands of men and women around the world, energizing them to take part in making Christ known in the many situations to which priests and religious have no entrée. The movement has experienced weaknesses as well as strengths, and in the United States it is smaller than it used to be. But the Cursillo movement continues to have an impact, and much can be learned from it. The national center of the movement in the United States can be contacted at (214) 339-6321 (www.natl-cursillo.org).

DON'T WORRY ABOUT ME

Questions to Begin

15 minutes
Use a question or two to get warmed up for the reading.

---

1   When have you gotten some good news from a relative or friend you had been worried about?

---

2   When you have to give a person painful news, do you tend to
❏ get right to the point?
❏ try not to give the bad news all at once?
❏ pass over unpleasant details?
❏ ask someone else to do it?
❏ mumble?

Opening the Bible

2 | *Acts 28:16–31;*
Philippians 1:12–26

5 minutes
Read the passage aloud. Let individuals take turns reading paragraphs.

The Reading: Acts 28:16–31; Philippians 1:12–26

Paul's Situation in Luke's Words

Acts 28:16 When we came into Rome, Paul was allowed to live by himself, with the soldier who was guarding him.

17 Three days later he called together the local leaders of the Jews. When they had assembled, he said to them, "Brothers, though I had done nothing against our people or the customs of our ancestors, yet I was arrested in Jerusalem and handed over to the Romans. 18 When they had examined me, the Romans wanted to release me, because there was no reason for the death penalty in my case. 19 But when the Jews objected, I was compelled to appeal to the emperor. . . . 20 For this reason therefore I have asked to see you and speak with you, since it is for the sake of the hope of Israel that I am bound with this chain." 21 They replied, "We have received no letters from Judea about you, and none of the brothers coming here has reported or spoken anything evil about you. 22 But we would like to hear from you what you think, for with regard to this sect we know that everywhere it is spoken against."

23 After they had set a day to meet with him, they came to him at his lodgings in great numbers. From morning until evening he explained the matter to them, testifying to the kingdom of God and trying to convince them about Jesus both from the law of Moses and from the prophets. 24 Some were convinced by what he had said, while others refused to believe. . . .

30 He lived there two whole years at his own expense and welcomed all who came to him, 31 proclaiming the kingdom of God and teaching about the Lord Jesus Christ with all boldness and without hindrance.

Paul's Situation in Paul's Words

Philippians 1:12 I want you to know, beloved, that what has happened to me has actually helped to spread the gospel, 13 so that it has become known throughout the whole imperial guard and to everyone else that my imprisonment is for Christ; 14 and most of the brothers and sisters, having been made confident in the Lord by my imprisonment, dare to speak the word with greater boldness and without fear.

^{15} Some proclaim Christ from envy and rivalry, but others from goodwill. ^{16} These proclaim Christ out of love, knowing that I have been put here for the defense of the gospel; ^{17} the others proclaim Christ out of selfish ambition, not sincerely but intending to increase my suffering in my imprisonment. ^{18} What does it matter? Just this, that Christ is proclaimed in every way, whether out of false motives or true; and in that I rejoice.

Yes, and I will continue to rejoice, ^{19} for I know that through your prayers and the help of the Spirit of Jesus Christ this will turn out for my deliverance. ^{20} It is my eager expectation and hope that I will not be put to shame in any way, but that by my speaking with all boldness, Christ will be exalted now as always in my body, whether by life or by death. ^{21} For to me, living is Christ and dying is gain. ^{22} If I am to live in the flesh, that means fruitful labor for me; and I do not know which I prefer. ^{23} I am hard pressed between the two: my desire is to depart and be with Christ, for that is far better; ^{24} but to remain in the flesh is more necessary for you. ^{25} Since I am convinced of this, I know that I will remain and continue with all of you for your progress and joy in faith, ^{26} so that I may share abundantly in your boasting in Christ Jesus when I come to you again.

Questions for Careful Reading

10 minutes
Choose questions according to your interest and time.
(The questions refer only to the reading from Philippians.)

1 What do verses 12 and 13 suggest about the kind of relationship Paul had with the men who were guarding him?

2 In verse 15, Paul refers to "some" who proclaim the gospel from envy. In what city do they seem to be doing this?

3 Paul makes a short, pithy statement about himself in verse 21. On the basis of his other statements, how would you unpack his meaning?

4 What kind of information about himself does Paul give in this passage? Why would he tell the Philippians what he does? What kind of information about himself does he not give? Why doesn't he give it?

5 In what ways does this passage illustrate an earlier statement of Paul's about knowing "what is best" (1:10)?

A Guide to the Reading

If participants have not read this section already, read it aloud. Otherwise go on to "Questions for Application."

Acts 28:16–31. Luke's description of Paul under house arrest shows him using every opportunity to help people come to know Jesus, his Lord. At the end of this scene we might imagine Paul seeing his visitors to the door, then asking an assistant to take dictation as he begins to compose his letter to the Philippians.

Philippians 1:12–14. Paul reassures the Philippians that things at his end are going well. He does not say that he is comfortable (perhaps he isn't), but he mentions that his imprisonment has advanced the gospel. Paul assumes that the Philippians are as intensely concerned about the Christian mission as he is.

My wife and I have found that when we move to a new home, our little Shih Tzu, Rupert, quickly brings us into contact with our neighbors. Paul discovered that his "chains" (translated "imprisonment" in 1:13–14) were useful for meeting people. Through his imprisonment, many of the nine thousand soldiers in the emperor's elite guard have heard about Jesus. In addition, his chains have spurred Christians in Rome to shake off timidity and proclaim Jesus more openly. Perhaps they thought, *If Paul can suffer for the gospel, hey, why can't I? Since his freedom has been curtailed, I'll have to pick up where he left off!*

1:15–18. Some Christians in Rome are not put off by Paul's imprisonment because they know he has been "put," or "assigned," there by the Lord (1:16). Others apparently regard his imprisonment as a sign of God's disfavor and use it as an opportunity to outshine him by their own evangelistic efforts. On the assumption that Paul is as self-concerned as they are, these Christians think their evangelistic success will rile him. Paul recognizes their motives, which are seriously deficient (he places "rivalry" and selfish "ambition" on his lists of serious vices—translated "envy" and "strife" in Romans 1:29 and Galatians 5:20–21). "But so what?" he responds. "So long as the gospel is preached, I am happy." The attempt to bother Paul fails, for he is more concerned about the advancement of Jesus than about his own advancement.

In Paul's view, God can and does use flawed human beings to advance his cause. While Paul prefers purity of motives, he does not insist on it as a requirement for Christian service. Paul implicitly offers himself to the Philippians as a model for how to relate to ambitious, self-serving members in their own community: he encourages them to focus on achieving the common goals of Christian mission rather than on criticizing one another's motives. Working together for Christ requires looking beyond our fellow Christians' imperfect attitudes, knowing that our own motivations are far from perfect.

1:18–20. Contrary to what we might expect, Paul is not in an agony of uncertainty about his trial, even though a possible death sentence hangs over him. In court his main concern will not be to establish his innocence in terms of Roman law but to bear witness to Jesus Christ. The "deliverance" Paul hopes for (1:19) is not acquittal but rescue from any weakness that would lead him to be disloyal to Christ. Although the verdict of the trial is in doubt, Paul can rejoice because he is certain that he will have the assistance of the Spirit to enable him to remain faithful to Christ. And he is confident that whether the Roman court decides for or against him, he will ultimately be vindicated by God (verse 20).

1:21–26. Paul sees a bright side to his imprisonment, to the rivalry of brethren, and even to his approaching trial; he knows that all these misfortunes can play a part in making Jesus known. Paul's desire for people to know about Jesus is rooted in an even deeper desire—the desire simply to be with Jesus. This is why Paul does not, like most of us, favor earthly life over death. Because death is the doorway into Christ's presence, Paul would prefer to die, or at least, if it were up to him, he would find it hard to choose between life and death (1:21–23). "Since my earthly life is focused on serving Christ, and death will only bring me closer to him, why should I be afraid of death?" Paul asks. Paul is not actually facing a choice between life and death: it is the court that will either sentence him to death or release him. But he is showing the Philippians why he does not quail at the prospect of execution.

Nevertheless, Paul suspects that Christ has unfinished business for him in this world and that he will be released to carry it out (1:24–26).

Questions for Application

40 minutes
Choose questions according to your interest and time.

1 When has the example of someone else's service to God strengthened your faith and energized you to serve? How has seeing someone's patient endurance of sickness or other suffering affected your faith and hope in God?

2 How might the restrictions on your own freedom—imposed by your job or studies, living situation or family responsibilities, lack of money, ill health, youth, or age—create an opportunity for communicating the gospel to another person?

3 Is it possible to have entirely pure motives, to be free of self-interest, in serving God and other people? When have you become aware that your motives for doing good were mixed? What did you do in response to this realization?

4 Paul's tolerance of the work of Christians with mixed and even base motives is striking. Do you welcome and praise the good that other people do, even when there seems to be some degree of self-interest in their efforts?

5 How would you complete the statement "For me, living is . . ."? What are you living for? What is the controlling desire of your life?

6 How does a person come to have his or her vision of life centered on Jesus Christ, as we see in Paul? Do you want to have that kind of relationship with Jesus?

7 What practical step could you take to direct your life more toward the goal of bearing fruit for Christ?

Bible discussion leaders are ordinarily not Scripture experts, nor do they need to be. Their function is to coordinate the group's search for meaning and inspiration in the word of God.

Jerome Kodell, O.S.B., *The Catholic Bible Study Handbook*

Approach to Prayer

15 minutes
Use this approach—or create your own!

◆ Let someone in the group pray
this prayer aloud. Take a few
minutes for silent reflection.
Close by praying the Our Father
together.

Lord, you have given us freedom
and curtailed our freedom.
You give us the power to love;
yet you have placed us within the
    limitations
of our energies and talents,
our finances,
our health and age.

Lord, we wish to serve you.
We wish to share your love
with those around us.
So we offer ourselves,
with all our limitations,
to you.
As you used Paul's chains,
turn our limitations into
    opportunities
for sharing your word,
your love,
your kingdom.

Saints in the Making

Showing Love Where She Could

This section is a supplement for individual reading.

Paul was convinced that God had called him to be an apostle to the nations, yet he spent years confined as a prisoner. We might easily imagine that a man of Paul's energy level would feel intense frustration at being prevented from carrying out his mission. Yet he accepted his periods of captivity as part of his calling, using them as opportunities to bring the gospel to people whom he might otherwise never have met (see Acts 24, 26).

Imprisonment, of course, is not the only confinement that individuals suffer. Poor health is a more common limitation. There is a long tradition in the Church of men and women seeking opportunities to serve God amid the difficulties of sickness. One example is a French woman, Elizabeth Leseur (1866–1914), who was sick with hepatitis for much of her life and died of cancer. Her life was limited not only by ill health but also by her marriage. She and her husband, Felix, loved each other, but he was an atheist, and this curtailed her involvement in religious activities.

Nevertheless, Elizabeth was active within the narrow sphere that was open to her. She provided support to an orphanage. She decided that she would show kindness particularly to the irksome people in her life. "I want to have boundless charity especially toward those who do not attract me," she wrote in her diary. "Isolated from Christian conversation by her marriage," one writer recounts, "Elizabeth participated by prayer in the communion of saints." Above all, she prayed for Felix and offered the pain of her illnesses to God as part of her prayer.

When Elizabeth died, Felix read her diary and was astonished by the depth of her love for God and for him that he discovered there. This discovery accomplished what no rational argument for the existence of God had been able to do. He came to faith in God and became not only a Christian but also a Dominican priest. In his later years he traveled throughout Europe making his wife's spirituality known. Felix himself became a confirmation of Elizabeth's belief that "through the divine action even our slightest pains, our least sorrows, can reach out to souls both near and distant and bring them light and peace and holiness."

Week 3
DUAL CITIZENSHIP

Questions to Begin

15 minutes
Use a question or two to get warmed up for the reading.

1 When have words of encourage-ment from another person made an impression on you?

2 Judging from your own or your parents' marriage, what are the hardest issues for spouses to agree on?

Opening the Bible

5 minutes
Read the passage aloud. Let individuals take turns reading paragraphs.

The Reading: Philippians 1:27–2:11; John 13:1–17

The Imitation of Christ

Philippians 1:27 Only, live your life in a manner worthy of the gospel of Christ, so that, whether I come and see you or am absent and hear about you, I will know that you are standing firm in one spirit, striving side by side with one mind for the faith of the gospel, 28 and are in no way intimidated by your opponents. For them this is evidence of their destruction, but of your salvation. And this is God's doing. 29 For he has graciously granted you the privilege not only of believing in Christ, but of suffering for him as well—30 since you are having the same struggle that you saw I had and now hear that I still have.

2:1 If then there is any encouragement in Christ, any consolation from love, any sharing in the Spirit, any compassion and sympathy, 2 make my joy complete: be of the same mind, having the same love, being in full accord and of one mind. 3 Do nothing from selfish ambition or conceit, but in humility regard others as better than yourselves. 4 Let each of you look not to your own interests, but to the interests of others. 5 Let the same mind be in you that was in Christ Jesus,

6 who, though he was in the form of God,
   did not regard equality with God
   as something to be exploited,
7 but emptied himself,
   taking the form of a slave,
   being born in human likeness.
And being found in human form,
   8 he humbled himself
   and became obedient to the point of death—
   even death on a cross.

9 Therefore God also highly exalted him
   and gave him the name
   that is above every name,
10 so that at the name of Jesus
   every knee should bend,
   in heaven and on earth and under the earth,

^{11} and every tongue should confess
    that Jesus Christ is Lord,
    to the glory of God the Father.

The Master Performs a Humble Service

John 13:1 Now before the festival of the Passover, Jesus knew that his hour had come to depart from this world and go to the Father. Having loved his own who were in the world, he loved them to the end. ^{2} The devil had already put it into the heart of Judas son of Simon Iscariot to betray him. And during supper ^{3} Jesus, knowing that the Father had given all things into his hands, and that he had come from God and was going to God, ^{4} got up from the table, took off his outer robe, and tied a towel around himself. ^{5} Then he poured water into a basin and began to wash the disciples' feet and to wipe them with the towel that was tied around him. ^{6} He came to Simon Peter, who said to him, "Lord, are you going to wash my feet?" ^{7} Jesus answered, "You do not know now what I am doing, but later you will understand." ^{8} Peter said to him, "You will never wash my feet." Jesus answered, "Unless I wash you, you have no share with me." ^{9} Simon Peter said to him, "Lord, not my feet only but also my hands and my head!" ^{10} Jesus said to him, "One who has bathed does not need to wash, except for the feet, but is entirely clean. And you are clean. . . ."

^{12} After he had washed their feet, had put on his robe, and had returned to the table, he said to them, "Do you know what I have done to you? ^{13} You call me Teacher and Lord—and you are right, for that is what I am. ^{14} So if I, your Lord and Teacher, have washed your feet, you also ought to wash one another's feet. ^{15} For I have set you an example, that you also should do as I have done to you. ^{16} Very truly, I tell you, servants are not greater than their master, nor are messengers greater than the one who sent them. ^{17} If you know these things, you are blessed if you do them."

10 minutes
Choose questions according to your interest and time.

1 Identify Paul's references to unity. What is the relationship between unity among the Philippians and the humility that Paul encourages (2:3–4)?

2 Because Jesus was "in the form" of God and equal to God, his actions revealed God. Judging from Jesus' actions in Philippians 2:6–8, what kind of person is God? What qualities characterize God?

3 Who acts in Philippians 2:6–8? Who acts in 2:9–11?

4 The biblical scholar G. F. Hawthorne suggested that Paul composed the poem about Christ in 2:6–11 after meditating on John 13:3–17. What evidence in the texts might have led Hawthorne to this view?

5 In what way does Jesus (in John 13:1–10) show what it means to "regard others as better than yourselves" (Philippians 2:3)?

A Guide to the Reading

*If participants have not read this section already, read it aloud.
Otherwise go on to "Questions for Application."*

1:27–30. "Live your life" (1:27) is literally "live as citizens." The
Philippians know about citizenship. As citizens of a Roman colony
in Greece, they follow Roman laws and promote Roman interests in
a region far from the mother city. As Christians, they have an even
more important citizenship—in God's kingdom. Paul appeals to them
to follow its way of life and advance its cause. In their earthly city,
they should conduct themselves as citizens of their heavenly city.

Declaring that Jesus' lordship surpasses Caesar's brings
the Christians into conflict with their neighbors in their Rome-
oriented city (1:28). "Striving side by side" and "struggle" (1:27,
30) are part of their life. The Greek words carry the flavor of athletic
contests, even gladiatorial games. Citizenship in the heavenly city
is like sports: no pain, no gain. When God gives the gift of faith, a
share in Jesus' suffering for the kingdom comes as part of the
package (1:29). To embrace this suffering goes against human
tendencies. How is such a mental and emotional revolution possible? The question spurs us to read Paul's next words carefully.

2:1–5. The Philippian Christians will promote God's commonwealth only by following its way of life—living "in a manner
worthy of the gospel" (1:27). The heavenly city's civic life is geared
toward promoting God's glory rather than our own, seeking others'
welfare rather than our own. Thus Paul appeals to the Philippians
to treat one another with self-sacrificing love (2:1–11). Their pagan
culture admired glory seeking and praised ambition, so this call to
humble service was profoundly countercultural. Isn't it still?

Paul reminds the Philippians of their God-given resources
for this kind of living (2:1): love and consolation given by Christ,
the presence of the Holy Spirit, and their previous experiences of
God's care ("compassion and sympathy" is more literally "compas-
sions and sympathies"—the actual instances of God's compassion
and sympathy that they have experienced). "Draw on these
resources," Paul urges, "to build a community of mutual care."

Paul does not intend that Christians should hold identical
opinions (2:2), but that we should share a certain attitude, have
the same purpose, be united in a common commitment to the
gospel. To regard other people as "better" than ourselves (2:3)

does not mean cultivating a poor self-image. Paul's meaning is illustrated by some Franciscan friars of my acquaintance who care for homeless men in New York City. I doubt the friars regard the homeless men as holier or smarter than themselves; the friars probably try not to engage in such mental comparisons one way or the other. But they regard the homeless men as better than themselves in the sense that they treat them as deserving of care and attention, even at the cost of giving up families and careers of their own.

2:5–8. Jesus was the one who most fully regarded others as better than himself. He was "in the form of God"—clothed with God's splendor and majesty (John 17:5; Hebrews 1:3). But he did not look upon this divine condition as something to be used for his own advantage (2:6). He regarded divine power and glory as something to be used for the benefit of human beings (also his attitude toward earthly power and glory—Mark 10:42–45). By becoming a human being, Jesus showed that godlikeness is not a matter of grasping but of giving away. Jesus revealed God as the Giver Without Limit. The Greek text does not literally say that Jesus, "*though* he was in the form of God, did not regard equality with God as something to be exploited." The Greek can equally well be translated, "*precisely because* he was in the form of God, he did not regard equality with God as something to be exploited."

On our behalf, Jesus "humbled himself" (2:8). He voluntarily entered into the role of servant to us. In fact, he joined us in the lowest depths of degradation and anguish to which we humans can fall. He obeyed God's call to love, even to the point of death. His washing of his disciples' feet on the night before he died—a task reserved for slaves—illustrated in a simple gesture the self-relinquishing love through which he humbly and lovingly came to serve us (John 13).

2:9–11. In response to Jesus' obedience and humility, God raised him from death to glory and is now in the process of making Jesus the focal point of the whole universe. Ultimately all creation will acknowledge God by acknowledging Jesus, through whom God has made himself known as the Lord of love.

Questions for Application

40 minutes
Choose questions according to your interest and time.

1 In what ways does being active citizens of our heavenly commonwealth lead us to be active citizens of our earthly nation? Offer specific examples.

2 How are the values and lifestyle of the heavenly city different from those of the earthly city today? What implications does this have for how we should live out our heavenly citizenship? Again, offer specific examples.

3 In what ways do verses 2:1 and 2:5 speak of the resources that God gives us for making the personal transformation that Paul calls us to make in 2:1–11? How can we draw on these resources?

4 In your life, who has been a good example of the humble service that Paul speaks about in this passage? What have you learned from this person?

5 Reread 1:9–11 and 2:2–5.
Where is God inviting you
to make a change in your life
in response to Paul's words?
What step should you take?

6 In what situations do you tend
to focus on your own needs and
pay less attention to the needs
of people around you? Why?
What could you do to be more
attuned to others' needs in
these situations?

7 What does it mean to acknowledge in our lives that "Jesus
Christ is Lord" (2:11)? Does it
mean genuflecting when we
hear his name (2:10)? Try to be
personal and specific.

**Don't be afraid of pauses, or try to fill in silent moments. If you
give everyone time to think, they will bring up good points and ask
good questions.**

Neil F. McBride, *How to Lead Small Groups*

Approach to Prayer

15 minutes
Use this approach—or create your own!

◆ Begin with an Our Father. Have someone read aloud the following excerpt from a letter by St. Francis de Sales (d. 1622). Pause for silent reflection. End by praying Philippians 2:5–11 together.

I'm under such pressure that I don't have time to write you anything more than the great word of our salvation: *Jesus.* If only we could say this sacred name from our hearts just for once! Oh, what sweet balm it would spread to all the powers of our spirit! How happy we should be to have only Jesus in our understanding, only Jesus in our imagination. Jesus would be everywhere in us, and we would be everywhere in him. Let us try this: let us pronounce this sacred name as often as we can. And if for the present we can only stammer it, in the end we shall be able to say it properly.

A Living Tradition

"Jesus Christ Is Lord"

Philippians 1:27–2:11; John 13:1–17

3

This section is a supplement for individual reading.

Paul declares that God raised Jesus from the dead and gave him "the name that is above every name" (2:9). What name is that? Some scholars believe Paul means that God has given Jesus the name, or title, by which God himself is known in the Old Testament, that is, "Lord." This title, which expresses God's sovereignty and power, now belongs fully to Jesus, who is perfectly united with the Father.

Ultimately, the entire universe will recognize that Jesus is Lord over all (2:10–11). But in the meantime, his lordship is not publicly apparent. While there are signs of his rule, adequate for those who are willing to receive the gift of faith, much evidence seems to weigh against the assertion that Jesus is Lord. Suffering and injustice continue. Men and women have the freedom to flout his rule—and even we his followers do so when we fall into sin.

While Jesus' sovereignty is not yet fully manifested in the world, it is already celebrated in heaven (Revelation 5:6). On earth, we who believe in Jesus' lordship acknowledge it especially in the liturgy of the Eucharist. In the Eucharist, we enter into the worship of heaven (see Ephesians 2:6). Especially in the prayer of offering that follows the call to "lift up your hearts," we join in the worship of heaven in declaring that Jesus of Nazareth truly is, with the Father, sovereign over all. In the course of that prayer, we join our voices with the angels in proclaiming, "Holy, holy, holy, Lord, God of power and might. Heaven and earth are full of your glory," and we proclaim that Jesus shares in this sovereignty of God by continuing our song, "Blessed is he who comes in the name of the Lord"—a reference to Jesus, who has come as the perfect representation of God. The eucharistic prayer declares Jesus' death and resurrection and reaches its climax in the priest's proclamation, "Through him"—that is, through Jesus—"with him, and in him, in unity of the Holy Spirit, all honor and glory is yours, almighty Father, forever and ever." The entire people answer with a resounding acclamation: "Amen!" At this point, we celebrate now what the entire creation will acknowledge at the end of time: "Jesus Christ is Lord, to the glory of God the Father" (2:11).

Week 4

COMINGS AND GOINGS

Questions to Begin

15 minutes
Use a question or two to get warmed up for the reading.

1 When have you taken a trip to help someone in need?

2 Describe a situation in which you had serious cause for concern about someone who was traveling. How did things turn out?

3 When have you been particularly pleased and surprised to see someone return from a trip? When have you taken a trip to surprise someone?

5 minutes
Read the passage aloud. Let individuals take turns reading
paragraphs.

The Reading: Philippians 2:12–30

Paul Winds Up His Encouragement . . .

[12] Therefore, my beloved, just as you have always obeyed me, not only in my presence, but much more now in my absence, work out your own salvation with fear and trembling; [13] for it is God who is at work in you, enabling you both to will and to work for his good pleasure.

[14] Do all things without murmuring and arguing, [15] so that you may be blameless and innocent, children of God without blemish in the midst of a crooked and perverse generation, in which you shine like stars in the world. [16] It is by your holding fast to the word of life that I can boast on the day of Christ that I did not run in vain or labor in vain. [17] But even if I am being poured out as a libation over the sacrifice and the offering of your faith, I am glad and rejoice with all of you—[18] and in the same way you also must be glad and rejoice with me.

And Offers Two Examples

[19] I hope in the Lord Jesus to send Timothy to you soon, so that I may be cheered by news of you. [20] I have no one like him who will be genuinely concerned for your welfare. [21] All of them are seeking their own interests, not those of Jesus Christ. [22] But Timothy's worth you know, how like a son with a father he has served with me in the work of the gospel. [23] I hope therefore to send him as soon as I see how things go with me; [24] and I trust in the Lord that I will also come soon.

[25] Still, I think it necessary to send to you Epaphroditus—my brother and co-worker and fellow soldier, your messenger and minister to my need; [26] for he has been longing for all of you, and has been distressed because you heard that he was ill. [27] He was indeed so ill that he nearly died. But God had mercy on him, and not only on him but on me also, so that I would not have one sorrow after another. [28] I am the more eager to send him, therefore, in order that you may rejoice at seeing him again, and that I may be less anxious. [29] Welcome

him then in the Lord with all joy, and honor such people, [30] because he came close to death for the work of Christ, risking his life to make up for those services that you could not give me.

10 minutes
Choose questions according to your interest and time.

1 Despite the NRSV translation, verse 12 is ambiguous, because in Greek the word for "me" is lacking. If not himself, who is Paul urging the Philippians to obey?

2 In Paul's view, we and God both play a part in our doing his will (2:12–13). What understanding of God's part and ours can be gained from Paul's letter so far? See especially 1:6, 19–20; 2:1–2, 5.

3 What is God's "good pleasure" (2:13)?

4 Paul makes a negative reference to the Christians around him (2:20–21). In light of 1:14 (and 4:21), scholars are puzzled by his remark. What possible explanation would you suggest?

5 Compare Paul's attitudes toward death in 1:21 and 2:27. What can be learned from this comparison?

A Guide to the Reading

If participants have not read this section already, read it aloud. Otherwise go on to "Questions for Application."

2:12–13. Having introduced Jesus' example of humble love (2:5–11), Paul now completes his encouragement to the Philippians to live as citizens of God's kingdom (1:27). Paul's exhortation to "work out your own salvation" (2:12) speaks of a "continuous, sustained, strenuous effort," writes New Testament scholar Peter O'Brien. God's grace will bear fruit in us only if we make a vigorous response. God "energizes" us so that we may both will and do what he wishes (2:13). Here we touch on the mystery of cooperation between creator and creature. All our good resolutions and actions spring from God's grace, yet the deciding and doing are also up to us. We must work at our salvation, yet even the desire and power to do so come from God.

   "Fear and trembling" (2:12) is not terror at the thought of God's judgment but awe at his presence. God himself is working in us—what could be more awesome? (Compare 1 Corinthians 5:6–8; 6:15–20; 10:1–22; 11:27–32.) "Don't worry about whether *I'm* there to help and guide you, because *God* is working in you," Paul is saying. "Paul is far, but God is near."

   2:14–15. Paul urges the Philippians to avoid grumbling and bickering. Arguing and complaining are symptoms of not yet being willing to humble ourselves in service, not yet allowing God to reshape our willing and doing.

   2:15–16. If the Philippians do lead a life of humble service, they will offer a glimpse of God's light to their neighbors. As Christ demonstrated the true nature of God in the world, so now should the Philippians.

   2:17–18. Under the Mosaic covenant, a drink offering, or "libation," often accompanied grain and animal sacrifices (Numbers 15:1–10). Paul views his imprisonment as a drink offering that complements the Philippians' suffering for Christ, which is their own sacrifice to God. The Philippians do not seem to be facing martyrdom, so Paul's "being poured out" with them may not refer to martyrdom either. They and he are already offering themselves to God day by day as they grow in love and work together for the Christian cause.

2:19–24. While Paul expects the Philippians to live as citizens of the heavenly city in his absence, he is keeping an eye on them—as we see from his sending Timothy to find out how they are doing. Paul commends Timothy as one who exemplifies the imitation of Jesus. Timothy has "slaved" for the gospel (NRSV: "served"—2:22); Paul uses a Greek word from the same root for "slave," which earlier described Jesus' humble service (2:7).

2:25–30. Another imitator of Jesus is Epaphroditus, a Philippian Christian who brought the community's financial support to Paul. Epaphroditus risked his life to carry out his assignment (2:30). Perhaps he became ill on the journey to Rome but pressed on anyway. The Philippians probably expect him to stay on with Paul and continue to serve his needs, but Paul is sending Epaphroditus back to Philippi with a commendation that will protect him from any suspicions that he did not carry out his assignment well.

In Greek, the word for "minister" (2:25) is related to the words for "offering" (2:17) and "services" (2:30). These words referred to performing public services, generously supporting civic life. Thus, just as the Philippians' pagan neighbors demonstrated good citizenship by paying for temples to be built or sponsoring banquets at public festivals, the Philippian Christians are acting as good citizens of the heavenly city (1:27) by supporting the apostle.

Distressed (2:26) is a strong word (Mark uses the same Greek word to describe Jesus' agony in Gethsemane—Mark 14:33). Epaphroditus is sick with worry about the Philippians because he has heard that they are sick with worry about him. These people really love one another!

Death is the gateway to eternal life (1:21–23), but Paul still regards earthly life as a great blessing (2:27). He himself may long to depart and be with Christ (1:21), but he would have been crushed with sorrow if his friend Epaphroditus had departed! Gordon Fee remarks that we should keep Paul's reference to "one sorrow after another" in mind as we read his references to rejoicing. "Joy does not mean the absence of sorrow, but the capacity to rejoice in the midst of it."

Questions for Application

Choose questions according to your interest and time.

---

1 Paul speaks about God's leading us to will what is right and good (2:13). When have you experienced God giving you a new desire for what is good? Where in your life today would you like to have a greater desire for God's will? How might you pray for that?

---

2 In what situation in your life might it be helpful for you to remember that "it is God who is at work in you" (2:13)? How might you remind yourself?

---

3 Where do Paul's words in verse 14 apply to you? How could you take a more constructive approach to situations where you tend to argue and complain?

---

4 Paul has relied on Timothy's assistance. Who relies on your assistance? How could you serve that person in a deeper spirit of humility (see 2:2–4)?

5 When have you taken a risk for the sake of Christ? What did you learn from the experience?

6 Paul praises Timothy and Epaphroditus to the Philippians (2:20–22, 29–30). Why is it important to show honor? Who should be honored in the Church? How are people honored today in the Church? in your parish?

Let both your prayer and your reading of Scripture be constant; speak with God, then let him speak with you.

Cyprian of Carthage, *Letters*

Approach to Prayer

15 minutes
Use this approach—or create your own!

◆ Pray this prayer together.

> Lord, we believe that you have
> begun a good work in us,
> and we are confident that you
> will bring it to completion.
>
> Show us how to cooperate with
> you.
> Let your Spirit guide us
> in the awesome task of working
> out our salvation.
>
> May the attitude that Jesus had
> become our attitude,
> so that we may learn both to will
> and to carry out
> what you desire.

A Living Tradition

It's All Grace

This section is a supplement for individual reading.

A statement of Paul's in this week's reading was much quoted during a controversy that shook the Church in the fourth century—a controversy that continues to have significance for Christians. Paul states that "it is God who is at work in you, enabling you both to will and to work for his good pleasure" (2:13). In Paul's view, even our decisions to please God and all our actions that please him stem from God's activity in us. This understanding of God's thorough involvement in our response to him proved important in the fourth century when Christians had to evaluate the teaching of a British monk named Pelagius.

Pelagius wished to emphasize our human responsibility to respond to God's grace. We cannot just coast into heaven on God's mercy while continuing to sin, he said. Our responsibility for responding to God implies a capacity for good on our part, since we can be responsible for doing good and rejecting evil only if we are capable of choosing what is good and actually putting our decisions into practice. On these points, other Christians were in agreement with Pelagius.

Disagreement arose, however, over the way Pelagius explained God's part and our part. God gives us the capacity to do good, Pelagius claimed, and then leaves us to decide to do what is right and to carry out our decisions.

Hold on! cried a number of Christian teachers, including St. Augustine, a North African bishop who had learned from his own difficult experience of conversion to Christ how hard it can be to decide to turn from sin. Augustine argued that God does not just equip us to do good, by giving us a human nature with lots of constructive capacities, and then stand back and see how well we do. God joins us in our willing to do good and in our carrying it out. Augustine quoted Philippians 2:13 and then explained, "This is not because we ourselves do not actually will and work, but because we neither will nor perform any good without God's assistance."

The Church ultimately accepted Augustine's position. It affirmed that our entire response to God's call arises from the grace of God, who makes himself present in the depths of our being, leading us to desire what is good, to seek it, and to do it.

FOCUS ON JESUS!

Questions to Begin

15 minutes
Use a question or two to get warmed up for the reading.

1 When have you let yourself be convinced by a salesperson—and regretted it afterward?

2 What's your approach to parting with things?
- ❐ I really dislike accumulating things. If I haven't used something for a year, I throw it out.
- ❐ I enjoy sorting through stuff and getting rid of what I don't need.
- ❐ I like to hold a garage sale occasionally.
- ❐ I live surrounded by junk because I'm too busy to get rid of stuff I no longer need.
- ❐ You never know when you might need a typewriter or an old *National Geographic*.
- ❐ I've still got my science project from fifth grade. Would you like to see it sometime?

Opening the Bible

5 minutes
Read the passage aloud. Let individuals take turns reading paragraphs.

The Reading: Philippians 3:1–4:1

No Need to Embrace the Mosaic Law

3:1 Finally, my brothers and sisters, rejoice in the Lord.

To write the same things to you is not troublesome to me, and for you it is a safeguard.

2 Beware of the dogs, beware of the evil workers, beware of those who mutilate the flesh! 3 For it is we who are the circumcision, who worship in the Spirit of God and boast in Christ Jesus and have no confidence in the flesh—4 even though I, too, have reason for confidence in the flesh.

If anyone else has reason to be confident in the flesh, I have more: 5 circumcised on the eighth day, a member of the people of Israel, of the tribe of Benjamin, a Hebrew born of Hebrews; as to the law, a Pharisee; 6 as to zeal, a persecutor of the church; as to righteousness under the law, blameless.

7 Yet whatever gains I had, these I have come to regard as loss because of Christ. 8 More than that, I regard everything as loss because of the surpassing value of knowing Christ Jesus my Lord. For his sake I have suffered the loss of all things, and I regard them as rubbish, in order that I may gain Christ 9 and be found in him, not having a righteousness of my own that comes from the law, but one that comes through faith in Christ, the righteousness from God based on faith. 10 I want to know Christ and the power of his resurrection and the sharing of his sufferings by becoming like him in his death, 11 if somehow I may attain the resurrection from the dead.

Jesus Himself Is the Goal

12 Not that I have already obtained this or have already reached the goal; but I press on to make it my own, because Christ Jesus has made me his own. 13 Beloved, I do not consider that I have made it my own; but this one thing I do: forgetting what lies behind and straining forward to what lies ahead, 14 I press on toward the goal for the prize of the heavenly call of God in Christ Jesus. 15 Let those of us then who are mature be of the same mind; and if you think differently about anything, this too God will reveal to you. 16 Only let us hold fast to what we have attained.

Looking Forward to Being Transformed

[17] Brothers and sisters, join in imitating me, and observe those who live according to the example you have in us. [18] For many live as enemies of the cross of Christ; I have often told you of them, and now I tell you even with tears. [19] Their end is destruction; their god is the belly; and their glory is in their shame; their minds are set on earthly things. [20] But our citizenship is in heaven, and it is from there that we are expecting a Savior, the Lord Jesus Christ. [21] He will transform the body of our humiliation that it may be conformed to the body of his glory, by the power that also enables him to make all things subject to himself. [4:1] Therefore, my brothers and sisters, whom I love and long for, my joy and crown, stand firm in the Lord in this way, my beloved.

10 minutes
Choose questions according to your interest and time.

1 What is Paul talking about in 3:2–9? How would you summarize his argument?

2 What was Paul striving for before he became a follower of Jesus? What does he strive for now that he is one?

3 What statements by Paul earlier in the letter help explain what it means to "press on" to make Jesus your own (3:12)?

4 What does Paul mean by "forgetting what lies behind" (3:13)?

5 What is Paul referring to when he tells the Philippians to "hold fast" to what they have attained and to "stand firm" (3:16; 4:1)?

6 Why does Paul begin and end this section of his letter with references to joy (3:1; 4:1)?

A Guide to the Reading

If participants have not read this section already, read it aloud. Otherwise go on to "Questions for Application."

3:1–3. If any of the Philippians were dozing off as Paul's letter was being read aloud, I imagine they jerked awake at his sudden change of tone in verse 2. Some Christians—probably visitors to Philippi rather than members of the local church community—were claiming that non-Jewish Christians like the Philippians needed to complete their conversion to God by also embracing Judaism. Paul makes a strong rebuttal. He assures the Philippians that nothing is lacking in their relationship with God. They are already God's people—they are "the circumcision," he says, circumcision being the sign of membership in the community of God's people under the Mosaic covenant. Since they base their relationship with God on Jesus ("boast in Christ Jesus"), they do not need to follow the Mosaic law (place their "confidence in the flesh"). *Flesh* can be used here to refer to Judaism, because membership in the Jewish people usually comes with birth, which is a connection in the flesh, and is signified by circumcision, which is a mark in the flesh.

3:4–9. Paul can speak with authority about the claim that the Mosaic law would add something to non-Jewish Christians' relationship with God. From his own experience he can assure the Philippians that relating to God through Jesus is superior to relating to God through the Torah. Paul does not say that he found Judaism to be defective. But whatever the value of Judaism, Jesus surpasses it. Jesus surpasses absolutely "everything" (3:8).

Paul speaks as though following the Mosaic law and believing in Christ were mutually exclusive alternatives. In fact, Paul indicates that Jews who accept Jesus as the Messiah are free to follow the Mosaic law—as he himself did under certain circumstances (Acts 21:1–26; 1 Corinthians 9:20). But a person must make a choice about the *basis* of his or her relationship with God. A building can have only one foundation. If you call Jesus "Lord" (3:8), you receive the relationship with God that Jesus gives (the "righteousness . . . that comes through faith in Christ"—3:9). Your concept of righteousness becomes colored by Jesus' emphasis on love (see 1:9–11). You take Jesus as your model (2:5). You let his power transform you (3:10–11). All this will give your life a different shape than if you focused on fulfilling the Mosaic law.

3:10–11. We can see how deeply Jesus has affected Paul by Paul's desire to join Jesus in humble service, even in suffering. Note that Paul uses the present tense in verse 10: he is speaking not only about possible martyrdom at the end of his life but also of daily dying with Jesus. Note too the structure of verses 10 and 11: Paul's mention of sharing in Jesus' suffering is bracketed by references to Jesus' resurrection—the only source of power by which we can share in Jesus' sufferings.

3:12–14. Paul once strove intensely to obey the Mosaic law (3:5–6). Conversion to Jesus has not caused Paul to relax and just let God's grace do all the work; conversion has simply changed the direction of his striving. Now Paul desires to reach the goal of eternal life with Jesus. Striving to reach this goal, Paul has parted with "everything" (3:8)—his friends and reputation in Judaism, his comforts, even his freedom—without regret ("forgetting what lies behind"—3:13).

3:15–19. Paul returns to his warning about the Judaizing Christian missionaries. The Philippians should "hold fast" to what they have attained (3:16), not letting themselves be persuaded that they need to keep the Mosaic law. They should imitate Paul's Jesus-centered life (3:17). The Judaizing Christians are "enemies of the cross of Christ" (3:18) because their argument that Christians cannot be saved unless they follow the Mosaic law treats Jesus' saving death as insufficient (compare Galatians 2:21).

3:20–4:1. When Paul spoke about Jesus humbling himself and being glorified (2:5–11), he did not explain what this has done for us. Now Paul completes his thought. Jesus entered into our limited human life and inevitable death in order to overcome death for us and transform us into sharers in his divine life.

The Philippians, then, should live as citizens of heaven, for that is where their Savior is and where they hope to be. Just as Paul now counts his privileges and accomplishments in Judaism as things to be jettisoned (3:8–9), so the Philippians should count the privileges and accomplishments of their civic life in the Roman colony of Philippi as of no account. They should live fully for the heavenly commonwealth to which they now belong.

Questions for Application

40 minutes
Choose questions according to your interest and time.

1 What does it mean to lack confidence in one's relationship with God? What causes it? What has helped you grow in confidence in God's unconditional love for you?

2 What does it mean to experience the power of Jesus' resurrection (3:10) in our present life? How have you experienced the power of Jesus' resurrection?

3 Paul urges us to orient our lives toward fulfillment in Jesus (3:8–15, 20–21; see also 1:6, 9–11; 2:9–11, 16). What do you see as the main obstacles to your "forgetting what lies behind" (3:13)? Do you think this will become more difficult—or easier—as you get older? Why? What concrete steps can you take to direct your life toward the goal of final fulfillment in Jesus?

4 Reread verse 17. In what ways has imitation of other people shaped your relationship with God? Consider people you have heard or read about, as well as those you have known personally. Who do you regard as an especially suitable model for you to imitate? Why? What more could you do to imitate that person?

5 In contrast to the pattern of living that Paul has encouraged, the Judaizing Christian missionaries do not share in the sufferings of Christ and do not strive toward the heavenly goal (3:18–19). In what way might imitation of Christ's sufferings and an orientation toward heavenly life serve as criteria for evaluating the authenticity of various approaches to spirituality today?

Encourage each other to share feelings as well as ideas.

Oletta Wald, *The Joy of Discovery in Bible Study*

Approach to Prayer

15 minutes
Use this approach—or create your own!

◆ Read aloud the following passage about Columba Marmion, a monk in Belgium who became a noted spiritual director in the early twentieth century. Pause for reflection. End with an Our Father.

Blessed Columba Marmion gave a simple explanation of the importance of humility by contrasting two figures. On one side is the "praying" Pharisee of Jesus' parable, who proudly calls God's attention to his great achievements: "I fast twice a week; I give a tenth of all my income" (Luke 18:12). "God detests such self-righteous people, though they may be very correct," Abbot Marmion observed. On the other side is St. Paul, whose attitude was "I see my own righteousness as rubbish. My confidence is in Jesus, who alone gives value to what I do." Paul "glories not in his works but in his infirmities," said Marmion. "Such people are dear to God because they glorify his Son."

This section is a supplement for individual reading.

Thomas Aquinas, the great thirteenth-century theologian, was a perceptive and clear-thinking student of Scripture. Even after eight centuries, his interpretations of Scripture are well worth reading. St. Thomas offered instructive explanations of some puzzling points in this week's reading from Philippians.

3:1. Why does Paul preface his remarks about the Judaizing Christian missionaries with a reminder to rejoice? Thomas suggests that Paul's point is that we should "rejoice in the Lord, not in legal observances." In other words, Paul is not issuing a general encouragement to receive the Lord's joy; he is specifically urging us to find our joy in the Lord himself rather than in fulfilling the many ceremonial observances laid down in the Mosaic law.

3:3. What does Paul mean by not trusting "in the flesh"? Does he mean not being dominated by sinful desires? No, Thomas answers. "While in Paul's writings, 'the flesh' is sometimes to be understood as sinful fleshly desires, at other times it refers to fleshly observances." This, says Thomas, is Paul's meaning here: the keeping of the entire range of laws given as part of the covenant with Moses, which is signified by fleshly circumcision and involves "fleshly" matters, such as ceremonial purity and pure and impure foods.

3:6. How is it that Paul claims to have been "blameless" in Judaism, although elsewhere he admits that he was bound by sinful tendencies until he came into a relationship with Jesus (Romans 7)? Thomas explains that Paul was without fault in external matters, as were other upright people under the Mosaic covenant, such as Zechariah and Elizabeth (Luke 1:5–6). At the same time, Paul had not yet experienced the inner purification through Christ by which God causes his goodness to take root in the depths of the heart.

3:11. Why does Paul seem to speak as though he is doubtful that he will attain the resurrection? Thomas explains that Paul "says 'if somehow' on account of the difficulty, hardship, and labor involved." In other words, Paul's manner of speaking underlines the fact that while God's grace will get us to the goal, we must make vigorous efforts to cooperate with him.

THANKS FOR THE GIFT

Questions to Begin

15 minutes
Use a question or two to get warmed up for the reading.

1 Describe an incident in which you tried to help two people resolve a disagreement.

2 When have you received a particularly timely gift?

Opening the Bible

5 minutes
Read the passage aloud. Let individuals take turns reading paragraphs.

The Reading: Philippians 4:2–23

Keep On Keeping On

[2] I urge Euodia and I urge Syntyche to be of the same mind in the Lord. [3] Yes, and I ask you also, my loyal companion, help these women, for they have struggled beside me in the work of the gospel, together with Clement and the rest of my co-workers, whose names are in the book of life.

[4] Rejoice in the Lord always; again I will say, Rejoice. [5] Let your gentleness be known to everyone. The Lord is near. [6] Do not worry about anything, but in everything by prayer and supplication with thanksgiving let your requests be made known to God. [7] And the peace of God, which surpasses all understanding, will guard your hearts and your minds in Christ Jesus.

[8] Finally, beloved, whatever is true, whatever is honorable, whatever is just, whatever is pure, whatever is pleasing, whatever is commendable, if there is any excellence and if there is anything worthy of praise, think about these things. [9] Keep on doing the things that you have learned and received and heard and seen in me, and the God of peace will be with you.

A Carefully Worded Thank-You

[10] I rejoice in the Lord greatly that now at last you have revived your concern for me; indeed, you were concerned for me, but had no opportunity to show it. [11] Not that I am referring to being in need; for I have learned to be content with whatever I have. [12] I know what it is to have little, and I know what it is to have plenty. In any and all circumstances I have learned the secret of being well-fed and of going hungry, of having plenty and being in need. [13] I can do all things through him who strengthens me. [14] In any case, it was kind of you to share my distress.

[15] You Philippians indeed know that in the early days of the gospel, when I left Macedonia, no church shared with me in the matter of giving and receiving, except you alone. [16] For even when I was in Thessalonica, you sent me help for my needs more than once. [17] Not that I seek the gift, but I seek the profit that accumulates to your account. [18] I have been paid in full and have more than enough; I am

fully satisfied, now that I have received from Epaphroditus the gifts you sent, a fragrant offering, a sacrifice acceptable and pleasing to God. 19 And my God will fully satisfy every need of yours according to his riches in glory in Christ Jesus. 20 To our God and Father be glory forever and ever. Amen.

Conclusion

21 Greet every saint in Christ Jesus. The friends who are with me greet you. 22 All the saints greet you, especially those of the emperor's household.

23 The grace of the Lord Jesus Christ be with your spirit.

10 minutes
Choose questions according to your interest and time.

1 How do Paul's words about sorrow in 2:27 help us understand what he says about rejoicing in 4:4?

2 What relationship might there be between the Philippians' rejoicing in the Lord and their letting other people see their gentleness (4:4–5)?

3 What does it mean to be content (4:11)? What does it mean to be content in plenty? What *is* the secret of being well fed and of going hungry that Paul has learned (4:12)?

4 Why does Paul refer to the members of the Christian communities in Philippi and Rome as "saints" (4:21–22)?

5 Looking back over the letter, how many times does Paul speak of being "in Christ"? of being "in the Lord"? What does he mean by these phrases? What does the frequency of these phrases suggest about his outlook on life?

A Guide to the Reading

If participants have not read this section already, read it aloud. Otherwise go on to "Questions for Application."

4:2–3. When Paul urged the Philippians to treat one another with humility and share a commitment to advancing the gospel (2:1–5), we may have detected a concern about divisions and rivalries among them. Our suspicion is confirmed as Paul now pleads with two women in the community to settle their differences. He appeals personally and directly to each, as though speaking face-to-face first to one, then to the other ("I urge . . . and I urge . . ."). We know nothing about their disagreement, but apparently these women filled roles of responsibility in the community—perhaps they were like Lydia, whose home was the original center of the Philippian church (Acts 16:13–15, 40).

4:4–5. Paul believes in rejoicing "always"—a difficult idea. He is no stranger to sorrow, even despondency (2 Corinthians 1:3–11). But when circumstances are bad, his approach is to rejoice "in the Lord." This does not mean pretending that bad things are okay (consider 2:26–27). From what Paul says in this letter (1:3–6, 18–19; 2:16–18; 3:20–21), we see that for him, rejoicing in the Lord means expressing confidence, even in painful situations, that God will complete his work in us and in the world.

4:6–9. Stop worrying, Paul adds—another difficult exhortation. But he shows us how: as one commentator remarks, "The way to be anxious about nothing is to be prayerful about everything." Paul does not promise that God will do whatever we ask of him. Jesus does urge us to expect to receive what we request in prayer (Mark 11:24). But in our weakness we often do not know how to pray or what to pray for (Romans 8:26). Nevertheless, God's peace is greater than our ability to comprehend his plans, and greater than our imperfect faith. If we put ourselves and our needs in his hands, his peace will encompass us (see John 20:19–20).

Making our requests to God "with thanksgiving" is not some clever tactic that obliges God to give us what we ask for because we have thanked him for it already. Judging from Paul's example, we are to offer thanksgiving not for what we expect but for what God has already given us—and not only for what he has given *us* but for what he has given others. Recall how Paul's thanksgiving was mainly for what God was doing with the Philippians, not for what the Philippians were doing for Paul (1:3–11). Paul's notion of thanksgiving moves us beyond self-centeredness. The more we are centered on God's concerns and the concerns of other people, the more we will experience the joy of God's kingdom. The celebration of the Eucharist, because it is the supreme expression of thanks to God for what he has done for the whole world through Jesus, trains us in the thankfulness that Paul has in mind.

4:10–14. In his thank-you to the Philippians for their financial gift, Paul tactfully avoids any appearance of dependence on their patronage, which might compromise his freedom to give them pastoral care. He focuses not on their money but on what it represents: their friendship with him and their partnership with him in advancing the gospel. "I could survive without the gifts," Paul says. "What is really important to me is your love."

Paul has mastered the art of self-sufficiency (being "content"—4:11). This was a common goal among pagan philosophers in the ancient world, but Paul gives it a distinctive twist. For him, contented *self*-sufficiency is based on *Christ*-sufficiency (4:13). Letting Christ be his all is the great "secret" Paul has learned (4:12).

4:15–20. Paul gratefully recalls the history of the Philippians' generosity to him without seeming to coax further gifts from them. He is glad for their kindness to him because it is, in effect, kindness to the Lord: it is "a fragrant offering, a sacrifice acceptable and pleasing to God" (verse 18). What was given to Paul was given to God. Thus their gifts produce an accrual of interest in their divine account (verse 17)—Paul's way of speaking about storing up treasure in heaven (Matthew 6:20; 19:21).

4:21–23. Paul's greeting from Christians in Rome mentions "those of the emperor's household." New Testament scholar Markus Bockmuehl points out that "the Philippians are a church in a Roman colony under persecution from their compatriots . . . while Paul similarly has suffered under Roman authorities both at Philippi and now at Rome. For both Paul and his friends, it will have been a source of hope and reassurance to know that the gospel was penetrating into the very heart of the Roman imperial apparatus."

Questions for Application

40 minutes
Choose questions according to your interest and time.

1 When have you allowed a disagreement or hurt feelings over a small matter to interfere with family life, with getting the job done at work, or with something else that was important? What did you learn from this experience?

2 Is it possible to avoid disagreements and hurt feelings with the people we are closely associated with? What are useful principles for dealing with these problems when they arise? How do the earlier parts of Paul's letter contribute to your understanding of how to reduce friction between people?

3 When have you been struck by the joy of someone who was suffering? What was the reason for their joy? When have you experienced joy in the midst of sorrow and difficulty? How can you share this joy with others?

4 What do you tend to worry
about? What helps you deal
with worry?

5 What kinds of true, honorable,
pleasing, excellent things do
you like to think about?

6 Paul learned how to be content
whether he had too much or too
little. Where do you need to
learn contentment? How does
affluence present a challenge
to contentment?

**Avoid the temptation to bring up those fascinating tangents that
don't really grow out of the passage you are discussing.**

Whitney Kuniholm, *John: The Living Word*

Approach to Prayer

15 minutes
Use this approach—or create your own!

◆ The introduction to this booklet made the following remark: "Reading Philippians is like meeting a saintly person: you find something about the person very appealing, yet also very disturbing, for even without the person saying a word, the person's life confronts you with the question 'Why shouldn't you be a saint too?'" Let participants mention, if they wish to, one way in which the letter to the Philippians challenges them to grow in holiness. Take a few minutes for prayer, allowing each person the opportunity to pray, silently or aloud, that God would have his way in his or her life. Close together with an Our Father, a Hail Mary, and a Glory to the Father.

Saints in the Making

The Strength to Sing

This section is a supplement for individual reading.

Following is a personal story by Patti Finn of Danbury, Connecticut.

Some years ago, my father developed terminal cancer. He and I had a wonderful relationship, and both of us loved Christian music. I play the guitar, and whenever I went to visit him I played for him and we sang together. I knew in my heart that when the time came, I would want to sing also at my dad's funeral. But my family and friends discouraged me. "You won't be able to do that when the time comes," they said.

Dad passed on and the time came to make the funeral arrangements. The funeral director told me that I would absolutely not be able to do the music for my father's funeral. He tried to convince me that no matter how much I wanted to do it, when I was standing in church it would be a different story. I cried, argued, and stormed out of his office. I went home with my heart aching, asking, "Lord, do you really want me to do this, or is everyone else right?" I opened my Bible trying to find comfort in God's word, as I often do. I opened to Philippians: "In him who is the source of my strength, I have strength for everything" (4:13). I knew that God had heard the cry of my heart and had answered my prayer.

As I stood in the church with my guitar and music, I knew everyone's eyes were on me, as if they were waiting for me to break down so they could say, "I told you so." But I held the Scripture in my heart and prayed, "In you, Lord, who are the source of my strength, I have strength for everything." I believed more than anything I ever believed in my life that God would indeed be my strength, and I would sing for my father's funeral. When the moment came, I sang beautifully, and I could see Dad smiling. Afterwards, people asked, "How did you ever do that?" It was an opportunity for me to say, "I couldn't do it, but God could!"

I have since made Philippians 4:13 an integral part of my life. Whenever I'm doubtful or feel myself struggling, I cling to Paul's words and know that God is my only strength; apart from him I can do nothing.

Not "Pay, Pray, and Obey"

A surprising aspect of Paul's letter to the Philippians is that he takes so long to get around to thanking them for their financial support. The Philippian community was by no means wealthy. Describing their generosity in another letter, Paul spoke of their "extreme poverty" (2 Corinthians 8:2). Now they have sent him another substantial gift, yet it is not until the end of his letter that Paul mentions it explicitly (4:10–20). What an unusual thank-you note!

Some scholars find it hard to believe that Paul did in fact leave his thanks until so late in the letter. They speculate that the letter as we have it is a somewhat amateurish stitching together of three shorter letters by Paul, one of which was 4:10–20. In this original note, the theory goes, he got right to the point of thanking the Philippians for their support.

In recent years, however, several scholars have argued that Philippians is indeed a single letter, not a pastiche of several letters, and that Paul did in fact leave his thanks for the end. They offer various explanations for this. Perhaps Paul wished his thanks to ring in the Philippians' ears as they finished reading his letter aloud at their assembly. Perhaps he avoided a focus on money because he did not wish to reduce his friendship with them to a utilitarian level.

In any case, other portions of the letter clearly show that Paul did not regard the Philippians mainly as a source of financial support. He speaks of their "sharing" in the cause of the gospel with him (1:5). The Greek word means "active partnership." The Philippians were like business partners with Paul in the enterprise of making Jesus known.

While Paul had a clear sense of his own calling to be an apostle, he did not think that meant he should do all the work of Christian mission while others merely provided the financing. Paul would have thought that any parish in which the laypeople were expected merely to "pay, pray, and obey" was seriously deficient.

Certainly Paul saw himself as the leader and guide for the Philippians. The whole letter shows him teaching them about Christian life, and we see him attempting to facilitate reconciliation in their community (4:2–3). But his leadership did not displace others' initiative—far from it. Paul commends one of the Philippians for his wholehearted, risk-taking involvement in Christian service (2:25–30). He singles out others as "coworkers" who have "struggled beside" him "in the work of the gospel" (4:3). He refers to the Philippians literally as his "copartners in suffering" (4:14).

Nowhere do we get the impression that the Philippians let Paul do all the evangelistic work while they passively soaked up his teaching and pastoral care and got on with their personal lives. They did not view Christianity as a matter of their private devotion, with the work left to religious professionals. The Philippians saw themselves as responsible for advancing the gospel. The letter shows apostle and people working together to make Christ known— an excellent example of cooperation for clergy and laity today.

Paul does not actually speak of the Philippians "preaching" the gospel. It is unlikely that they devoted themselves full-time to evangelizing. Probably they advanced the gospel as they went about their ordinary occupations and activities. In fact, this is how Paul himself must often have spread the word about Jesus. In most of his travels he supported himself by working as a tent maker (Acts 18:1–3). We may picture him in his craftsman's booth in the marketplace, running his knife quietly through a piece of canvas or leather while engaging a purchaser in conversation about God.

Reading Philippians leads me to fantasize about a letter sent out today by a bishop to laypeople who have contributed to a fund-raising appeal. The bishop expresses how happy he is about the many ways that he and the people of the diocese are working together to make Jesus known, bringing principles of justice to bear in public life, providing services to people in various kinds of need. He reflects at length on the deepening relationship with Jesus that he and the laypeople are experiencing as they labor side by side. He tells them a little about himself. Then, only in the final paragraph, almost as a minor matter, he acknowledges their tax-deductible contribution. Their financial support, after all, is the smallest part of their involvement with the mission of the church.

Wouldn't that be fine?

Was Paul Anti-Jewish?

On first reading, chapter 3 of Philippians *seems* to denigrate Judaism. To interpret Paul's words as a condemnation of Judaism, however, would be to seriously misunderstand him. It is true that Paul says nothing positive about Judaism in this passage. But that is only to be expected, given his purpose. He is reassuring the Christians in Philippi, who had been pagans, that they do not need to embrace Judaism in order to be in a right relationship with God. Jesus is all they need. Naturally, in order to convey this reassurance, Paul emphasizes the advantages of faith in Jesus. We would hardly expect him at this moment to discourse on the glories of the Mosaic law. From his other writings, however, we know that Paul greatly valued the history of God's dealings with Israel, the Scriptures of Israel, and the worship of the Jewish people in the temple (Acts 13:16–43; 21:17–26; Romans 9–11).

Paul has outgrown his earlier understanding of Judaism, but he does not say he did so because he discovered shortcomings in Judaism. Rather, when Jesus appeared to him, Paul realized that he had to choose between continuing to focus his life on the Mosaic law and beginning to focus his life on Jesus. He could not do both, because his life could not have two centers. It was in order to follow Jesus that Paul left behind much that he had known as God-given and good in Judaism. Paul came to see that the advantage of being in a relationship with Jesus is so inconceivably great that not just Judaism but "everything" else seems by comparison so much "rubbish" to be discarded (3:8). Paul's statement does not disparage Judaism; it exalts Jesus. "Jesus is of *such* tremendous value," Paul declares, "that compared with him *Judaism itself* seems like trash to be abandoned!"

If we look closely at Paul's apparently anti-Jewish statements, we will see that none of them unambiguously expresses criticism of Judaism itself:

- ◆ Paul's abusive language (3:2) is not directed against Jewish missionaries urging non-Jews to embrace Judaism but against Jewish-*Christian* missionaries urging Christians to add Jewish observances to their faith in Christ. In Philippians 3, Paul expresses not his opinion of Jews and Judaism but only his opinion of Christians who do not grasp that Jesus is sufficient for our relationship with God. Such Christians are "enemies of the cross of Christ" (3:18).

◆ While Paul asserts that Christians are God's people (3:3), he does not say that Jews who do not accept Jesus as Messiah have ceased to be God's people. Paul does not deal here with the question of the continuing value of Judaism for those who practice it now that the Messiah has come. Indeed, no New Testament writer takes up this question. (The bishops at Vatican Council II [1962–65] did speak positively on this subject: "Although the Church is the new people of God, the Jews should not be presented as repudiated by God" [*Declaration on the Relationship of the Church to Non-Christian Religions,* section 4]).

◆ Paul's words in 3:9 ("not having a righteousness of my own that comes from the law, but one that comes through faith in Christ, the righteousness from God based on faith"—NRSV) may seem to characterize Judaism as a self-righteousness approach to God. But the Greek may also be translated "not having as my kind of righteousness that which comes from the law but that which comes through faith in Christ, the kind of righteousness that comes from God by faith." Thus Paul is not making a contrast between *self*-righteousness through Judaism and *God-given* righteousness through Christ. He is saying that he left behind the righteousness that comes through keeping the law in order to embrace the *greater* right-eousness that comes through Christ. Paul's point is not to offer a negative evaluation of Judaism or of the quality of his life as a Jew (3:6) but to emphasize the tremendous power of righteousness and resurrection that he encountered when he met Christ (3:10–11). Paul regarded both Torah and Christ as gifts of God (the qualities of Judaism that Paul enumerates in 3:5 were all gifts to be received, not points of self-accomplishment). Only he came to see that God's gift in Christ surpasses his gift through Moses.

Suggestions for Bible Discussion Groups

Like a camping trip, a Bible discussion group works best if you agree on where you're going and how you intend to get there. Many groups use their first meeting to talk over such questions. Here is a checklist of issues to consider, with bits of advice from people who have experience in Bible discussions. (A planning discussion will go more smoothly if the leaders have thought through the following issues beforehand.)

Agree on your purpose. Are you getting together to gain wisdom and direction for your lives? to finally get acquainted with the Bible? to support one another in following Christ? to encourage those who are exploring—or reexploring—the Church? for other reasons?

Agree on attitudes. For example: "We're all beginners here." "We're here to help each other understand and respond to God's word." "We're not here to offer counseling or direction to each other." "We want to read Scripture prayerfully." What do *you* wish to emphasize? Make it explicit!

Agree on ground rules. Barbara J. Fleischer, in her useful book *Facilitating for Growth,* recommends that a group clearly state its approach to the following:

- Preparation. Do we agree to read the material and prepare answers to the questions before each meeting?
- Attendance. What kind of priority will we give to our meetings?
- Self-revelation. Are we willing to gradually help the others in the group get to know us—our weaknesses as well as our strengths, our needs as well as our gifts?
- Listening. Will we commit ourselves to listening to one another?
- Confidentiality. Will we keep everything that is shared *with* the group *in* the group?
- Discretion. Will we refrain from sharing about the faults and sins of people outside the group?
- Encouragement and support. Will we give as well as receive?
- Participation. Will we give each person time and opportunity to make a contribution?

You could probably take a pen and draw a circle around *listening* and *confidentiality.* Those two points are especially important.

The following items could be added to Fleischer's list:

◆ Relationship with parish. Is our group part of the adult faith-formation program? independent but operating with the express approval of the pastor? not a parish-based group?

◆ New members. Will we let new members join us once we have begun the six weeks of discussions?

Agree on housekeeping.

◆ When will we meet?

◆ How often will we meet? Meeting weekly or every other week is best if you can manage it. William Riley remarks, "Meetings once a month are too distant from each other for the threads of the last session not to be lost" (*The Bible Study Group: An Owner's Manual*).

◆ How long will meetings run?

◆ Where will we meet?

◆ Is any setup needed? Christine Dodd writes that "the problem with meeting in a place like a church hall is that it can be very soul-destroying" given the cold, impersonal feel of many church facilities. If you have to meet in a church facility, Dodd recommends doing something to make the area homey (*Making Scripture Work*).

◆ Who will host the meetings? Leaders and hosts do not necessarily have to be the same people.

◆ Will we have refreshments? Who will provide them?

◆ What about childcare? Most experienced leaders of Bible discussion groups discourage bringing infants or other children to adult Bible discussions.

Agree on leadership. You need someone to facilitate—to keep the discussion on track, to see that everyone has a chance to speak, to help the group stay on schedule. Rena Duff, editor of the newsletter *Sharing God's Word Today,* recommends having two or three people take turns leading the discussions.

It's okay if the leader is not an expert regarding the Bible. You have this booklet, and if questions come up that no one can answer, you can delegate a participant to do a little research between meetings. It's important for the leader to set an example of listening, to draw out the quieter members (and occasionally restrain the more vocal ones), to move the group on when it gets stuck, to remind the members of their agreements, and to summarize what the group is accomplishing.

Bible discussion is an opportunity to experience the fulfillment of Jesus' promise "Where two or three are gathered in my name, I am there among them" (Matthew 18:20). Put your discussion group in Jesus' hands. Pray for the guidance of the Spirit. And have a great time exploring God's word together!

Y ou can use this booklet just as well for individual study as for group discussion. While discussing the Bible with other people can be a rich experience, there are advantages to individual reading. For example:

◆ You can focus on the points that interest you most.
◆ You can go at your own pace.
◆ You can be completely relaxed and unashamedly honest in your answers to all the questions, since you don't have to share them with anyone!

My suggestions for using this booklet on your own are these:

◆ Don't skip "Questions to Begin." These questions can help you as an individual reader warm up to the topic of the reading.
◆ Take your time on "Questions for Careful Reading" and "Questions for Application." While a group will probably not have enough time to work on all the questions, you can allow yourself the time to consider all of them if you are using the booklet by yourself.
◆ After reading the "Guide to the Reading," go back and reread the Scripture text before answering the "Questions for Application."
◆ Take the time to look up all the parenthetical Scripture references.
◆ Since you control the pace, give yourself plenty of opportunities to reflect on the meaning of Philippians for you. Let your reading be an opportunity for these words to become God's words to you.

Resources

Bibles

The following editions of the Bible contain the full set of biblical books recognized by the Catholic Church, along with a great deal of useful explanatory material:

- ◆ The Catholic Study Bible (Oxford University Press), which uses the text of the New American Bible
- ◆ The Catholic Bible: Personal Study Edition (Oxford University Press), which also uses the text of the New American Bible
- ◆ The New Jerusalem Bible, the regular (not the standard or reader's) edition (Doubleday)

Books

- ◆ Markus Bockmuehl, *The Epistle to the Philippians* (Peabody, Mass.: Hendrickson Publishers, 1998).
- ◆ Raymond E. Brown, "The Letter to the Philippians, in "*An Introduction to the New Testament* (New York: Doubleday, 1997), 483–501.
- ◆ Gordon D. Fee, *Paul's Letter to the Philippians* (Grand Rapids, Mich.: W. B. Eerdmans Publishing Co., 1995).

How has Scripture had an impact on your life? Was this booklet helpful to you in your study of the Bible? Please send comments, suggestions, and personal experiences to Kevin Perrotta, c/o Trade Editorial Department, Loyola Press, 3441 N. Ashland Ave., Chicago, IL 60657.